For my wife Ellen and our Little Bear - C.M.

To R., A., and K., who inspire worlds within worlds. - L.W.

FARMER BEAR'S GARDEN

By Chris Magee

Illustrated by Lezlee Ware

One spring day when the sun was bright and the air was warm,
Farmer Bear said, "Come along, Little Bear! It's time to plant the garden!"

Little Bear jumped out of his chair and helped gather the tools and seeds.
Once everything was ready, they headed out to the backyard.

First, Farmer Bear measured out the rows.

Then he dug some holes and Little Bear dropped in the seeds.

They covered them with just the right amount of dirt and sprinkled on some water.

"What now, Dad?" Little Bear asked.

"Now we wait and see what happens," Farmer Bear replied.

Every morning Little Bear ran outside to look, but it was always the same — an empty patch of dirt.

"You have to be patient, dear," Momma Bear said. But it was so hard.

Then one day it rained all morning
and all afternoon, and Little Bear
had to stay inside.

"Wake up, Little Bear," Farmer Bear said the next morning. "I have something to show you!" They went out to the garden, and everywhere Little Bear looked he could see little green plants beginning to poke up from the ground.

"Wow, look at them all!" Little Bear exclaimed.

All through the summer, Farmer Bear and Little Bear worked in the garden.

They watered the plants,
picked off the bugs,
and pulled out the weeds.

And every day the plants
grew a little more.

Soon the days started getting cooler, and then one morning
Farmer Bear said, "Come along, Little Bear, it's harvest time!"

They got some baskets and
Little Bear's wagon and went
to the garden. All around,
Little Bear could see ripe,
colorful vegetables.

All morning they worked. Little Bear picked the small things like peas and beans. Farmer Bear picked the bigger things like melons and corn.

Farmer Bear dug up orange carrots and brown potatoes. Little Bear picked bright red tomatoes and green peppers.

Slowly but surely their baskets filled up.

When they were done, Little Bear saw all they had grown with their hard work and couldn't believe it. "Wow, Dad, look at it all!" he exclaimed. "What are we going to do with everything?"

"Well, we can't eat all this ourselves," Farmer Bear said. "Why don't we share with our friends and neighbors?"

"That's a great idea!" Little Bear said. And so they went to the village.

Before long they met Mrs. Beaver. "Good afternoon," Farmer Bear said. "Would you and your family like some melons from our garden?"

Mrs. Beaver was excited at the thought of eating those sweet, juicy melons. "Thank you two so much!" she said. "I'd like to give you a gift in return. I'll send my boys over with some wood for your fireplace."

Farmer Bear thanked her and said goodbye.

Next they came to the Bird family. "Hello Mr. and Mrs. Bird," Little Bear said.

"We've grown some nice, big sunflowers in our garden and they're full of seeds. Would you like some?"

"That's so generous,"
Mr. Bird said.
"Our little ones
will love them."
Then Mrs. Bird gave them a wreath she had made.
"Please take this to add some cheer to your house."

"Thank you, Mrs. Bird,"
Farmer Bear said.
"I know the perfect
place for it."

A little while later they saw the Bunny family out working in their flower garden.

"Hi, Mrs. Bunny," Farmer Bear said. "We'd like to share some of our carrots with you."

"Oh, thank you, Farmer Bear," she replied. "I love fresh vegetables! Here, let me pick some flowers for your house."

Soon they reached Mrs. Hen and her chicks.
"Hi, Mrs. Hen," Farmer Bear said.
"I thought your chicks might like this corn."

"Thank you so much!" she said, taking the corn.
"They're eating me out of house and home."

As they walked away, Little Bear said,
"Dad, she didn't give us anything in return."

"We don't give gifts to get something back, son," Farmer Bear said. "We do it because they're our friends and we want to make them happy."

Little Bear thought that seemed like a pretty good reason.

They continued to meet other friends and neighbors and share their food. Some gave them small gifts in return. Some just gave smiles, but all were grateful. Little Bear felt good when they got home.

That night they sat down for dinner. Momma Bear cooked a delicious meal with some of the vegetables they grew. Little Bear couldn't wait to tell his mom about all the food they had given away and how happy everyone was.

After dinner they relaxed in the family room. Farmer Bear built a fire with the wood from the Beavers, and Momma Bear hung the wreath from the Birds on the wall. Mrs. Bunny's flowers were in a vase on the mantel.

Soon it was Little Bear's bedtime. As Mom and Dad tucked him into bed, he said, "Can I help you with your garden next year, Dad?"

"It's our garden now, son. And I'd love to grow it with you," Farmer Bear replied. "Good night."

That night Little Bear slept long
and deep after a hard day's work,
dreaming about sunny days and
yummy meals, and doing
it all again.

CPSIA information can be obtained
at www.ICGtesting.com
Printed in the USA
LVHW071501080421
683866LV00011B/396

9 781734 679618